MW01531337

Diapers to Diapers
and
Other Funny
Things

Pat Krause

authorHOUSE™

1663 LIBERTY DRIVE, SUITE 200
BLOOMINGTON, INDIANA 47403
(800) 839-8640
WWW.AUTHORHOUSE.COM

First published by AuthorHouse 10/06/05

ISBN: 1-4208-7896-4 (sc)

Printed in the United States of America
Bloomington, Indiana

This book is printed on acid-free paper.

This book is dedicated
to my late husband
EUGENE L. KRAUSE
who was really
the inspiration for this book
and to my mother,
the late
DOROTHY MARTINEZ
who enjoyed
my warp sense of humor
and of course to
all of the older people
I know and love

This book could not have been
completed without the
endless effort of the
Illustrator, CRAIG PATTERSON
NU PRINTS www.nuprints.com

special mention to
FELIX MARTINEZ, my dad
ROY HINES
&
DEBBIE BOWLING
for their support and encourgement

FOREWORD
...Is that something like foreplay?

During my "menopausal" year, I cried, and cried, and cried. Those "hot" flashes made the South Texas July heat seem like a cold snap. Then there was that wonderful senior weight gain—you know that "it's never going to happen to me" weight gain.

After all was said and done, I have come to the conclusion that growing older was really hilarious—that if you do not laugh about it now there would not be enough Prozac in the world to help!

During my late husband's lengthy illness, we found reasons to laugh about the changes affecting his life. The laughter helped him cope. In fact several of these ideas were his. Now that it is my turn and I am growing older and a little slower, I appreciate those humorous moments.

I tell young people, when I was 18, I'd primp and comb and make-up for hours on end. Then I turned 30 and I realized that I only had so much to work with and to try to improve. Now I look in the mirror and just say "thank you." Being alive is just as nice with a size 35 waist, boobs hanging low enough to contribute to that 35 waist, and a few wrinkles. In fact it is nicer because I don't have to impress anyone or fit into anything. While I was never a raving beauty I'm still fairly attractive just in case anyone wants to look.

It is comforting knowing that when watching TV and the Super Models with their perfect make-up, fantastic body and full hair, that we're all headed in the same direction. So "don't hate me because I'm beautiful" (remember that commercial), just love me because I'm old.

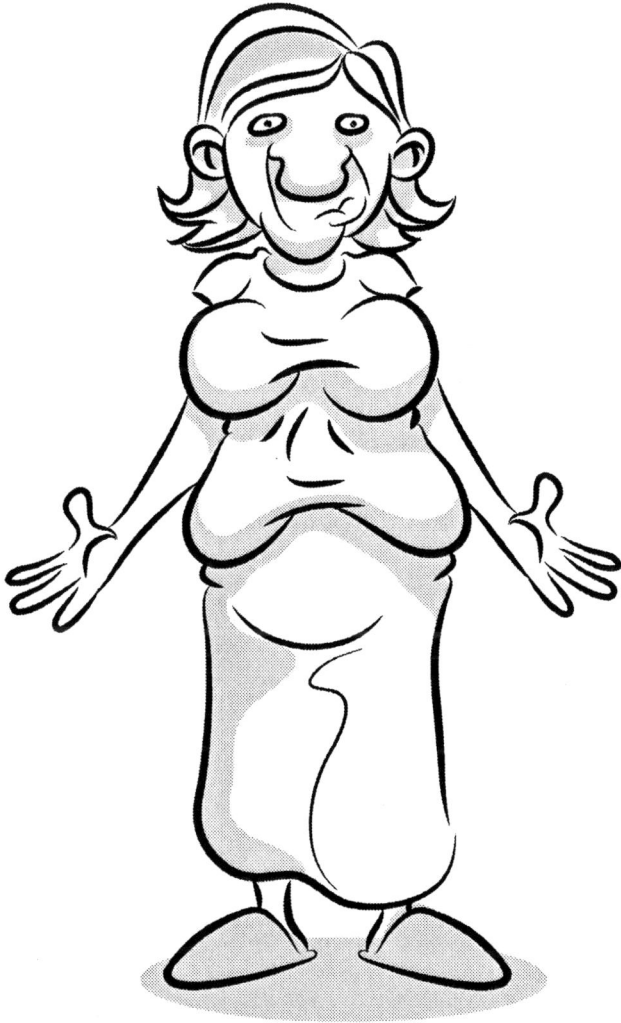

Some things just can't keep up!

Help!
They've fallen and can't get up!

Help!
He's fallen and can't get up!
Late Husband, Gene

Are they real or are they silicone?

Side effects of Viagara

Side effects of Viagara

SENIOR DRAG RACING

Late Husband, Gene

MAN'S SECOND CHILDHOOD

Debbie B.

TOP SPEED...5 MPH
Late Husband, Gene

Thing about being bald...
You don't know when to stop
washing your face!

Why can't this hair be on my head?
Roy

MAN'S MIDLIFE CRISIS

WOMAN'S MIDLIFE CRISIS

MAN'S BEST FRIEND

WOMAN'S BEST FRIEND

She says...Hold that thought!

BAD HAIR DAY

NOT FAIR...NOT FAIR!!

Roy

MAN'S HELL
Debbie B.

WOMAN'S HELL
SORRY MADAM...
NO CHOCOLATE HERE

Debbie B.

Sorry Sir...No Beer Here.
Remember this is YOUR Hell?
Debbie B.

WHAT HAPPENED??

Why didn't someone tell me women
could grow this much hair?

He use to watch me shave...
Now all he can do is watch
me shine my shoes!
Late Husband, Gene

MENOPAUSAL SURVIVAL HAT

WORKING WOMAN'S
MENOPAUSAL BRIEFCASE
Debbie B.

Is it tremors or Parkinson...
At this age who can tell!

It's only high octane gas!

I just hate it when these
things get in the way!
Debbie B.

You know you're getting old when
you dress younger than your daughter

Hi! I'm here for my hundred thousand mile check up!

Run for the hills...
I think he's gonna blow!

Well...I'm not TOTALLY bald!

Best Dressed Man...
You've Seen Him!

When He Still Thinks He Is a Size 32

I bet the guy who invented
Spandex is saying, "Wow, I didn't
know it could do that."

You do what you gotta do

SENIOR FASHION
STATEMENT

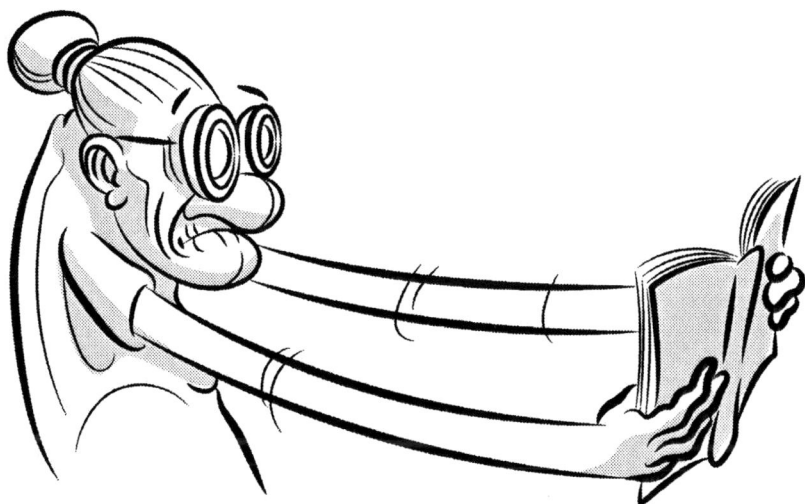

I don't need glasses...
My arms are just too short!

I CAN SEE PERFECTLY FINE!

When your next prescription
will be a seeing eye dog!

OLD AGE SEX

Hurry, let's get out of here.
We're not that old!

HAPPY HOUR

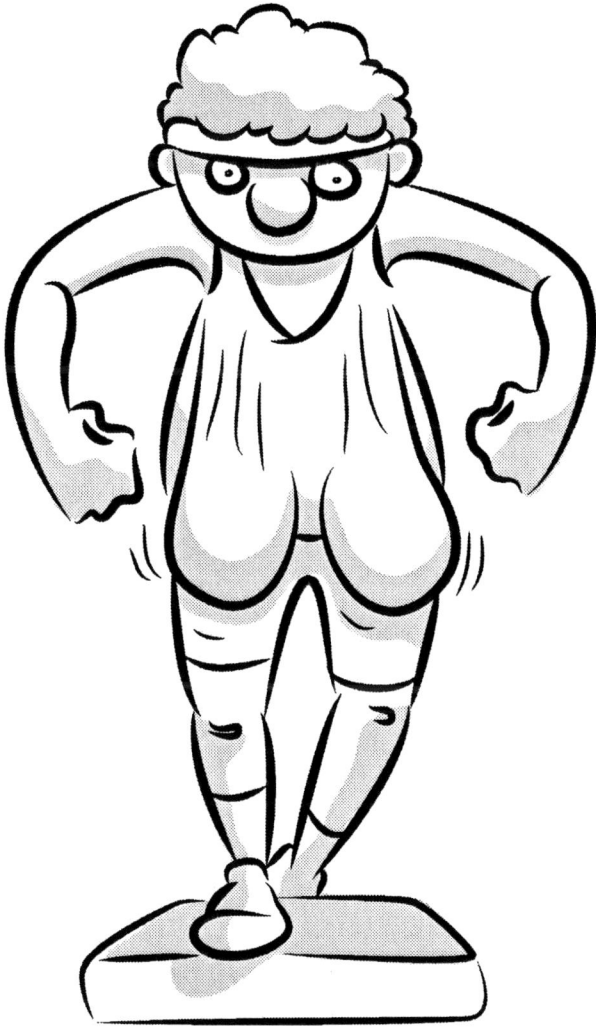

Body Out Of Shape?

When you're embarrassed
by your parents...
Leave them at home!

NOBODY LOOKS ANYWAY

Really... It's just a hot flash!

I DON'T need glasses!

50th HIGH SCHOOL REUNION

When you're old comparing
ailments is the life of the party

Yes, they ARE stud earrings, but
at this age everything droops!

MODERN CONVENIENCES
OF OLD AGE

WOMAN'S OLD AGE SYMBOL

Don't laugh...
Take a good look!

And the best part... there
are no side effects...Just
unplug in the morning

TIME TO DIET

Don't leave home without them!

SIMPLE ADORNMENT...
THE LATEST ALL IN ONE...
HAT, GLASSES,
EARRINGS, HAIR!

2006 MODELS
Debbie B.

Life can't get any easier than this...
The all in one fashion accessory...
Hat, glasses, earrings, & hair!

The box say if it stays like this for four hours, seek medical attention!

I can't go anywhere. My bra won't fit! You and your bright ideas for sexual enhancement!

I'm sorry...I wasn't thinking!

SPORTS GEAR...
FOR YOUR BALLS?

He wouldn't let me do it
while he was alive!
Late Husband, Gene

Jokes

I realized one day that I'm not really fat...I'm just too short.

You know that commercial that says if you are trying to loose 5 or 10 vanity pounds, this pill is not for you. I wish I only had 5 or 10 pounds to loose.

Remember the old movie about the pods that when you slept your body would be taken over by the "body snatchers". Well, I've decided they can have mine.

You know that one pounder Hungry Man TV Dinner. They ought to make a version for us women—Middle Age Lean Cuisine. And why is it they get to eat a pound for dinner and all we get is diet meals?

My late husband use to say what doesn't hurt, doesn't work!

I usually drive because my boyfriend's driving makes me nervous. He brags that he hasn't had an accident. I tell that's because everyone gets out of his way!

Have you noticed that as men get older, they THINK they get hornier!

I once read a book titled, *You and Your Mind.* I chuckled...I didn't know I still had one!

Have you noticed that by the time you really know how to do it...You can't.

Happiness is remembering your name. Happiness is remembering where you're going. Extreme happiness is remembering where you've been.

I've noticed that my elevator doesn't go to the top floor, heck it doesn't even know it has a top floor.

About the Author

The author, Pat Krause, is a native Texan living in the hill country. She developed a sense of humor after a few tragedies in her life—the loss of her daughter in 1997, the loss of her husband in 2002, and the loss of her mother in 2004. Over the years she developed the philosophy of laughter! She realized that each tragedy was just what was planned and that to survive and live happily, it took seeing things in a funny way. Laughter keeps things in perspective, keeps you young and just makes life fun! Now Pat helps others see just how funny it is to get old—no more tears, no more "I wish". Pat knows that life is an appreciation for what is today—that beauty is what is inside and that the outward stuff is just stuff. There are no more pretentious or plastic worries. You are happy to be just as you are because you are beautiful! Be grateful for what is... that we are all just where we are suppose to be. If we knew what we know now in our younger days, things would be so much easier. But that is the learning process—God's Plan!

Printed in the United States
37604LVS00005BB/358-1008

9 781420 878967